My Christmas 2020

 # Time Capsule

*A groundbreaking book to help your child remember and cherish
their unique journey through 2020*

Janani Balachander

Neil & Anika - Thank you for filling our lives with love and laughter.

Avyukt - Aunty loves you.

To our parents, families and our Guru:
we are eternally grateful for your love, support and guidance in our lives.

Janani & Bala

This book was first published in 2020 by Janani Balachander, trading as JB Picture Books.
For business enquires please contact: jbpicturebooks@gmail.com

ISBN: 978-1-9160287-7-7

Text & Illustrations copyright (c) Janani Balachander, 2020

Wow! What a year this has been...!

So let's begin with marking the months you were mostly home.

JAN   FEB   MAR

APR   MAY   JUN

JUL   AUG   SEP

OCT   NOV   DEC

What did you learn this year?

1.

2.

3.

4.

Write everything you disliked about this year.

1.

2.

3.

4.

Now cut along the dotted line, crumple it, and bin it.

Looks like you enjoyed 2020. How about helping the ants enjoy it too.

Now cut along the dotted lines and help the ants reach the cakes.

Now that you crushed 2020, can you write the things that made you happy?

1.

2.

3.

4.

People who made 2020 good for you...

Thank these amazing people by designing badges for them.

Dear _____

YOU ARE
a STAR

Dear _____

Dear _____

Dear _____

Need more of these? Go to the last page...

Well done! Now why don't we do some ~~mindfullness~~ mindlessness exercises before we jump into the other activities?

Scribble away with both your hands at the same time.

Right <u>Right</u>

Stop when you have no more space left.

Left

Now, put your face down, outline your face and give yourself features!

Hold as many crayons as you can and scribble away until it makes you happy.

Close your eyes and run your pencil through all the circles below.

Try doing it in one go!

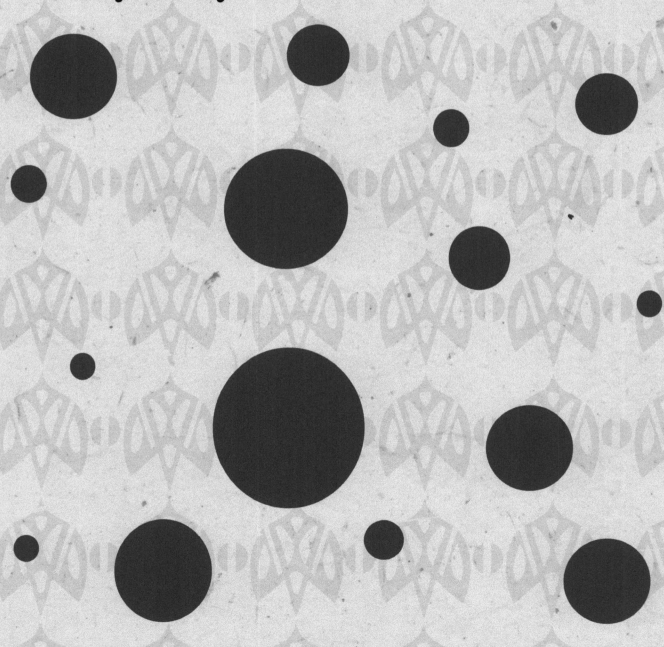

Great, now let the

games begin...

Complete the Santa drawing below.

You have great coloring skills.
Can you design an ornament and hang
it on your Christmas tree?

Did you like that? Why don't you color these two?

Santa is visiting lots of kids today. Help him sanitize his hands.

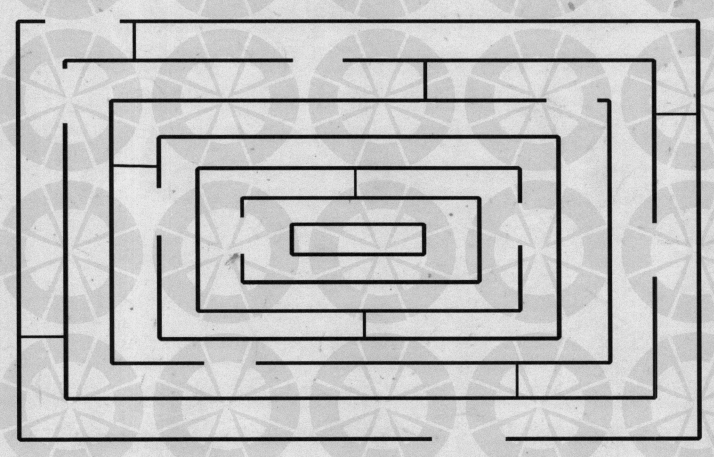

Flip back to the previous pages and see if you can spot these elves.

Hint: This elf is in your tree.

Santa needs to change his mask every four hours. Can you design a mask and leave it with his cookies and milk?

✂ -

Santa is traveling around the world. Where do you want to go next year?

Boarding Pass

Date _____

Destination _____

Gate number	Boarding Time	Seat number
B4	12:00	4A

Name of Passenger

_____

From

_____

To

_____

Boarding Pass

Date _____

Destination _____

Gate number	Boarding Time	Seat number
32A	18:00	5B

Name of Passenger

_____

From

_____

To

_____

Now, let's make some memories...

Who did I wake up to on Christmas ?

Draw thier faces or stick in some pictures.

What I ate for Christmas 2020...

My favorite present this year is...

Three things I am grateful for this year:

1.

2.

3.

Three things my family is grateful for:

1.

2.

3.

Write a letter to your future self about this year!

Write about the lovely and not-so-lovely things you experienced in 2020. Write about your dreams for the future.

Dear Me,

Here is your envelope:

2.Apply glue on the blue area and press hard.

1. Fold along this line.

Here is your envelope:

To,

_____

_____

_____

_____

Draw
a
stamp

My Christmas 2020

Paste pictures from your celebrations.

Stick your envelope with the letter here.

Congratulations!
Your time capsule is now
complete.

If you have enjoyed creating this time capsule, share your joy with us at: jbpicturebooks@gmail.com

Other books by the team:

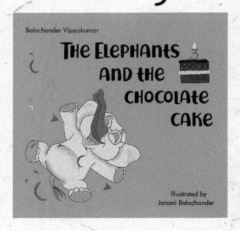

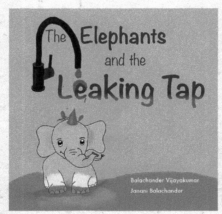

available at

amazon

CPSIA information can be obtained
at www.ICGtesting.com
Printed in the USA
BVHW022153041220
594952BV00032B/849